Anonymous

Raise the Flag

And Other Patriotic Canadian Songs and Poems

Anonymous

Raise the Flag
And Other Patriotic Canadian Songs and Poems

ISBN/EAN: 9783744678247

Printed in Europe, USA, Canada, Australia, Japan

Cover: Foto ©Thomas Meinert / pixelio.de

More available books at **www.hansebooks.com**

RAISE THE FLAG

AND OTHER

PATRIOTIC CANADIAN SONGS

AND POEMS.

" Shall we break the plight of youth
And pledge us to an alien love?
No! We hold our faith and truth,
Trusting to the God above.
Stand, Canadians, firmly stand
Round the flag of Fatherland!"
—LESPERANCE

Toronto
ROSE PUBLISHING COMPANY.
1891.

CANADA ! Maple-land ! land of great mountains !
Lake-land and river-land !   Land 'twixt the seas !
Grant us, God, hearts that are large as our heritage,
Spirits as free as the breeze.

Grant us thy fear that we walk in humility,
Fear that is rev'rent—not fear that is base—
Grant to us righteousness, wisdom, prosperity,
Peace—if unstained by disgrace.

Grant us thy love and the love of our country ;
Grant us thy strength, for our strength's in thy name ;
Shield us from danger, from every adversity,
Shield us, Oh Father ! from shame !

Last born of nations !   The offspring of freedom !
Heir to wide prairies, thick forests, red gold !
God grant us wisdom to value our birthright,
Courage to guard what we hold !

PREFACE.

In February last a deputation consisting of a large number of influential men, of all parties and creeds, waited upon the Minister of Education, to advocate the raising of a flag on the school houses on national anniversaries. The Toronto School Board had already taken steps towards the same end, and the movement has since been spreading throughout the Province. The anniversary of the battle of Queenston Heights was most successfully commemorated in all the public schools of Toronto, on the 13th October last, large numbers of essays upon the battle being written in all the schools. The *Empire* newspaper has also offered a large flag to the school in each county which produces the best essay on the subject of "Raising the Flag."

As an encouragement to the children, who have written the best essays in each school, and who would otherwise receive no recognition of their success, a few loyal Canadians have compiled (and subscribed the cost of producing) this little collection of Patriotic Songs and Poems, as the most appropriate remembrance to be given to the scholars who have written the best essays on these subjects.

The songs and poems selected, although few in number, strike the keynote of Canadian history and sentiment. Among them may be found the romantic and touching story of the foundation of this Province by the United Empire Loyalists ; who, driven from their homes in the revolted colonies, disappeared in the gloomy recesses of the unbroken wilderness of Upper Canada, and amid the most terrible hardships, privations, and trials,

"Won from the Canadian wild
A home on British lands."

The guiding principle of these men was contained in the text "Fear God, honor the King." Piety and loyalty and steadfast endurance being their distinguishing characteristics.

From the pathos of this period we come to the war of 1812, when once more these men and their sons had to take up arms to defend the humble homes they were carving out of the forest. A scant people, then only 70,000, they faced enormous odds, and in three long years of incessant war, drove back invasion after invasion of vastly superior numbers. The triumphant martial spirit of a victorious people breaks out exultingly in the poems of this war—Queenston Heights, the Capture of Detroit, and the brave exploit of Laura Secord being described in stirring verse.

There is nothing so striking in Canadian poetry as the great change that has come over it during the last few years. The tone of confidence in our country, the buoyant faith in our great future, the deep feeling of loyalty to Canada and the Empire, that is shown in all the fugitive pieces of the last five years is most remarkable. Mr. Wm. D. Lighthall, to whose excellent collection of " Songs of our Great Dominion," this work is indebted for several extracts, notices this fact in his introduction, but since he wrote, the change is even more marked. Still we notice the same dominant idea of fearing God and honoring the king. The piety of the later poems is as marked as the loyalty.

Canada has been compelled to defend her frontiers in open war in 1775 and in 1812-15, and from fillibusters in 1837 and 1838, and again in 1866 and 1870. Every generation of our people for one hundred years has seen Canadian lives given up freely in defence of her soil and institutions. Our territory has been diminished by unfair treaties ; and trade regulations and restrictions, and fishery disputes, have been used to retard our progress or coerce us into annexation. Yet with it all our poems are singularly free from unfriendliness. There is no tone of aggression, but a steadfast determination to trust in God and stand firm for the right. The only tinge of bitterness that is shown, here and there, is towards those of our own people who lack faith in our future. The feeling towards our neighbors is shown in Mr. Cockin's lines :

> " Peace, an' they will, nay more, a friendly hand,
> But not one foot of our Canadian land."

Grateful acknowledgment is hereby given to the authors, whose poems are here published with the object of spreading among the children of our land those loyal and patriotic sentiments which animated our fathers and helped them to defend and hand down to us the rights and privileges which we now enjoy.

CONTENTS.

RAISE THE FLAG

AND OTHER

Patriotic Canadian Songs and Poems.

RAISE THE FLAG.

BY E. G. NELSON.

RAISE the flag, our glorious banner,
  O'er this fair Canadian land,
From the stern Atlantic Ocean
  To the far Pacific strand.

Chorus.

  Raise the flag with shouts of gladness,
    'Tis the banner of the free !
  Brightly gleaming, proudly streaming,
    'Tis the flag of liberty !

Raise the flag o'er hill and valley,
  Let it wave from sea to sea ;
Flag of Canada and Britain,
  Flag of right and liberty !—*Chorus.*

Raise the flag, and with the banner
  Shouts of triumph let us raise ;
Sons of Canada will guard it,
  And her daughters sing its praise.—*Chorus.*

Raise the flag of the Dominion,
  That the world may understand,
This will be our ensign ever
  In our broad Canadian land.—*Chorus.*

Raise the flag ! who dare assail it,
  Guarded by the Empire's might ?
Raise the flag of our Dominion,--
  Stand for country, God, and right !—*Chorus.*

CANADA TO THE LAUREATE.

BY " FIDELIS."

> " And that true North, whereof we lately heard
> A strain to shame us ! Keep you to yourselves,
> So loyal is too costly ! Friends, your love
> Is but a burden ; loose the bond and go !
> Is this the tone of Empire ? "
>
> TENNYSON'S *Ode to the Queen.*

WE thank thee, " Laureate," for thy kindly words
Spoken for us to her to whom we look
With loyal love, across the misty sea ;
Thy noble words, whose generous tone may shame
The cold and heartless strain that said " Begone,
We want your love no longer ; all our aim
Is riches—*That* your love can *not* increase."
Fain would we tell them that we do not seek
To hang dependent, like a helpless brood
That, selfish, drag a weary mother down ;
For we have British hearts and British blood
That leaps up, eager, when the danger calls !
Once, and again, our sons have sprung to arms
To fight in Britain's quarrel—*not our own*—
And drive the covetous invader back,
Who would have let us, peaceful, keep our own,
So we had cast the British name away.
Canadian blood has dyed Canadian soil
For Britain's honour, that we deemed our own ;
Nor do we ask but for the right to keep,
Unbroken still, the cherished filial tie
That binds us to the distant sea-girt isle
Our fathers loved, and taught their sons to love,
As the dear home of freemen brave and true,
And loving *honour* more than ease or gold !

THIS FAIR CANADIAN LAND.

BY H. C. COCKIN.

How fair is this land which the might of our fathers
   Bequeathed to their children to have and to hold ;
From lonely Belleisle, where Atlantic foregathers,
   To Mackenzie that down thro' the ages has roll'd !
Yes, fair is the land, with its great inland waters,
   Vast links, forg'd of God, in the national chain,
That shall teach our brave sons and our virtuous daughters
   To attune heart and voice to the patriots' strain ;
      Then patriots say, Shall alien footsteps stand
      In triumph on this fair Canadian land ?

O, Britain, dear Britain, ever glorious nation !
   Whose strong arm in peace nigh engirdles the earth :
Canadians turn yet, aye, in proud exultation,
   To the mother of nations that gave to them birth.
Oh, where be the hearts that in trait'rous illusion
   Would barter for pottage a birthright so fair ;
On each be the brand of dark shame and confusion,
   And the stews of sedition his crime-haunted lair.
      God make his hope but as the rope of sand,
      And one and indivisible this land.

Of the people who dwell in the land on our borders
   We are kinsmen—not lovers—and can never be one ;
Apart lies our future, and He will afford us
   The help of His arm till our destiny's done.
We like them, but yet are their ways not as our ways ;
   There, the marriage-tie's but a tale that 'is told ;
There, the Bench and the Forum are equally powerless
   When Justice and Honour are ravish'd by gold.
      Peace, an' they will—nay more—a friendly hand,
      But not one foot of our Canadian land !

AN ODE FOR THE CANADIAN CONFEDERACY

BY CHARLES G. D. ROBERTS.

AWAKE, my country! the hour is great with change!
  Under this gloom which yet obscures the land,
From ice-blue strait and stern Laurentian range,
  To where giant peaks our western bounds command,
A deep voice stirs, vibrating in men's ears
  As if their own hearts throbbed that thunder forth,
A sound wherein who hearkens wisely hears
  The voice of the desire of this strong North,—
        This North whose heart of fire
        Yet knows not its desire
  Clearly, but dreams, and murmurs in the dream.
The hour of dreams is done! Lo, on the hills the gleam!

Awake, my country! the hour of dreams is done!
  Doubt not, nor dread the greatness of thy fate.
Tho' faint souls fear the keen confronting sun,
  And fain would bid the morn of splendour wait;
Though dreamers, rapt in starry visions, cry—
  " Lo, yon thy future, yon thy faith, thy fame!"
And stretch vain hands to stars, thy fame is nigh,
  Here in Canadian hearth, and home, and name;—
        This name which yet shall grow
        Till all the nations know
  Us for a patriot people, heart and hand,
Loyal to our native earth—our own Canadian land.

O, strong hearts, guarding the birthright of our glory,
  Worth your best blood this heritage that ye guard!
These mighty streams resplendent with our story,
  These iron coasts by rage of seas unjarred,—
What fields of peace these bulwarks well secure!
  What vales of plenty those calm floods supply!
Shall not our love this rough, sweet land make sure,
  Her bounds preserve inviolate, though we die?

O, strong hearts of the North,
Let flame your loyalty forth,
And put the craven and base to an open shame,
Till earth shall know the child of nations by her name !

EMPIRE FIRST.

BY JOHN TALON LESPERANCE—"*Laclède.*"

SHALL we break the plight of youth,
  And pledge us to an alien love ?
No ! We hold our faith and truth,
  Trusting to the God above.
        Stand Canadians, firmly stand,
        Round the flag of fatherland !

Britain bore us in her flank,
  Britain nursed us at our birth,
Britain reared us to our rank
  'Mid the nations of the earth.
        Stand, Canadians, firmly stand,
        Round the flag of fatherland !

In the hour of pain and dread,
  In the gathering of the storm,
Britain raised above our head
  Her broad shield and sheltering arm.
        Stand Canadians, firmly stand,
        Round the flag of fatherland !

O triune Kingdom of the brave !
  O sea-girt island of the free !
O Empire of the land and wave !
  Our hearts, our hands, are all for thee.
        Stand Canadians, firmly stand,
        Round the flag of fatherland !

THE MAPLE LEAF FOR EVER.

BY ALEX. MUIR.

In days of yore, from Britain's shore,
   Wolfe, the dauntless hero, came,
And planted firm Britannia's flag,
   On Canada's fair domain.
Here may it wave, our boast and pride,
   And, joined in love together,
The Thistle, Shamrock, Rose entwine
   The Maple Leaf forever!

At Queenston's Heights and Lundy's Lane,
   Our brave fathers, side by side,
For freedom, homes, and loved ones dear,
   Firmly stood and nobly died.
And those dear rights which they maintained,
   We swear to yield them never!
Our watchword evermore shall be,
   The Maple Leaf forever!

Our fair Dominion now extends
   From Cape Race to Nootka Sound;
May peace forever be our lot,
   And plenteous store abound;
And may those ties of love be ours
   Which discord cannot sever,
And flourish green o'er freedom's home,
   The Maple Leaf forever!

On merry England's far famed land,
   May kind Heaven sweetly smile;
God bless old Scotland evermore,
   And Ireland's Emerald Isle!
Then swell the song, both loud and long,
   Till rocks and forests quiver,
God save our Queen, and heaven bless
   The Maple Leaf forever!

UPON THE HEIGHTS AT QUEENSTON.

BY JAMES L. HUGHES.

UPON the heights at Queenston,
　One dark October day,
Invading foes were marshalled
　In battle's dread array ;
Brave Brock looked up the rugged steep,
　And planned a bold attack,
" No foreign flag shall float," said he,
　" Above the Union Jack ! "

His loyal-hearted soldiers
　Were ready, every one,
Their foes were thrice their number—
　But duty must be done.
They started up the fire-swept hill
　With loud resounding cheers,
While Brock's inspiring voice rang out—
　" Push on York Volunteers ! "

But soon a fatal bullet
　Pierced through his manly breast,
And loving friends, to help him,
　Around the hero pressed ;
" Push on," he said, "do not mind me,"
　And ere the setting sun,
Canadians held the Queenston Heights—
　The victory was won.

Each true Canadian patriot
　Laments the death of Brock.
Our country told its sorrow
　In monumental rock ;
And if a foe should e'er invade
　Our land in future years,
His dying words will guide us still—
　" Push on brave volunteers ! "

THE U. E. LOYALISTS.

An Extract from " The Hungry Year."

BY WM. KIRBY.

THE war was over, seven red years of blood
Had scourged the land from mountain top to sea ;
(So long it took to rend the mighty frame
Of England's empire in the western world)
Rebellion won at last, and they who loved
The cause that had lost, and kept their faith
To England's crown, and scorned an alien name,
Passed into exile, leaving all behind
Except their honour, and the conscious pride
Of duty done to country and to king.

Broad lands, ancestral homes, the gathered wealth
Of patient toil and self-denying years,
Were confiscate and lost ; for they had been
The salt and savor of the land ; trained up
In honour, loyalty, and fear of God.
The wine upon the lees, decanted, when
They left their native soil with sword belts drawn
The tighter ; while the women only wept
At thought of old firesides no longer theirs,
At household treasures reft, and all the land
Upset, and ruled by rebels to the king.

Not drooping like poor fugitives they came
In exodus to our Canadian wilds,
But full of heart and hope, with heads erect
And fearless eyes victorious in defeat.
With thousand toils they forced their devious way
Through the great wilderness of silent woods,
That gloomed o'er lake and stream, till higher rose
The northern star above the broad domain
Of half a continent, still theirs to hold,
Defend and keep for ever as their own,
Their own and England's to the end of time.

The virgin forests, carpeted with leaves
Of many autumns fallen, crisp and sear,
Put on their woodland state ; while overhead
Green seas of foliage roared a welcome home
To the proud exiles, who for empire fought
And kept, though losing much, this northern land
A refuge and defence for all who love
The broader freedom of a commonwealth
That wears upon its head a kingly crown.

Our great Canadian woods of mighty trees,
Proud oaks and pines that grew for centuries,
King's gifts upon the exiles were bestowed.
Ten thousand homes were planted ; and each one
With axe, and fire, and mutual help made war
Against the wilderness and smote it down.
Into the opened glades, unlit before,
Since forests grew and rivers ran, there leaped
The sun's bright rays, creative light and heat,
Waking to life the buried seeds that slept
Since time's beginning in the earth's dark womb.

The tender grass sprang up, no man knew how,
The daisies' eyes unclosed, wild strawberries
Lay white as hoar frost on the slopes, and sweet
The violets perfumed the evening air ;
The nodding clover grew up everywhere ;
The trailing rasp, the trefoil's yellow cup
Sparkled with dew drops, while the humming bees
And birds and butterflies, unseen before,
Found out the sunny spots and came in throngs.

But earth is man's own shadow, say the wise ;
As wisdom's secrets are twofold, and each
Responds to other both in good and ill ;
A crescent thought will one day orb to full,
And on the earth reflect true light of heaven.

But long and arduous were their labours ere
The rugged fields produced enough for all,
For thousands came ere hundreds could be fed ;
The scanty harvests gleaned to their last ear
Sufficed not yet, men hungered for their bread
Before it grew, yet cheerful bore the hard,
Coarse fare and russet garb of pioneers,
In these great woods, content to build a home
And commonwealth where they could live secure,
A life of honour, loyalty and peace

    *   *   *   *   *

* *   The world goes rushing by
The ancient landmarks of a nobler time,
When men bore deep the imprint of the law
Of duty, truth and loyalty unstained.
Amid the quaking of a continent
Torn by the passions of an evil time,
They counted neither cost nor danger, spurned
Defections, treasons, spoils ; but feared God,
Nor shamed of their allegiance to the king.

To keep the empire one in unity
And brotherhood of its imperial race,
For that they nobly fought and all but won,
Where losing was to win a higher fame
In building up our northern land, to be
A vast dominion stretched from sea to sea ;
A land of labour but of sure reward,
A land of corn to feed the world withal,
A land of life's best treasures, plenty, peace,
Content and freedom, both to speak and do ;
A land of men to rule, with sober law,
This Christian commonwealth, God's gift ; to keep
This part of Britain's empire next the heart,
Loyal as were our fathers, and as free.

THE BATTLE OF QUEENSTON HEIGHTS.

A Patriotic Poem Written on the Anniversary of that Great Victory.

BY WILLIAM THOMAS WHITE.

Ho ! ye who are Canadians, and glory in your birth,
Who boast your land the fairest of all the lands on earth,

To-night go home with cheerful heart and lay all care aside,
And set aglow your brightest lamps and throw the shutters
 wide.

Heap high with coal the fire, till its merriest sparks you win,
And send out all your messengers to call the neighbors in.

Then when the evening well is spent with feast and mirthful
 sound,
In circle deep about the hearth range girls and boys around.

Bring forth the book of heroes' deeds, and to your listening
 flock,
Read reverently of Queenston Heights and the death of
 Isaac Brock.

Oh, there are some amongst us who spurn the patriot's name,
Who say our country has no past, no heroes known to fame.

They talk of bold Leonidas who held the pass of blood,
And how Horatius Cocles braved swollen Tiber's flood.

They never tire of dark Cortez who spared nor blood nor
 tears,
Nor yet of Arnold Winkelreid, who broke the Austrian spears.

Their glory is of Waterloo, that crimson-memoried fight,
Of the "thin red line" of Inkerman and Alma's bloody
 height.

For Canada their voice is mute, yet history's pages tell
That braver blood was never spilt than where her heroes fell

To-day o'er Queenston's lofty heights the autumn sky is
    drear,
From drooping limbs the withering leaves hang bloodless,
    wan and sere.

From fertile sward the plough has gone, and from the field
    the wain,
In bursting barns the farmer views his wealth of garnered
    grain.

Those fields are sacred and that sward shall be Canadians'
    boast,
The spot where valor's few hurled back the dark invader's
    host.

The tale shall live while grow the trees, while rippling water
    runs,
Of fame's bright birth to Canada from the life-blood of her
    sons.

You know it well! The invaders crossed with the first grey
    dawn of light,
And foot by foot their numbers told and gained the stubborn
    height.

The guns are ta'en! on Dennis' flank the reinforcements
    pour,
While from the battery on the hill the crashing round-shot
    tore.

And backward, surely backward, the patriot heroes move,
With death to left and death to right and death on high
    above.

But, hark! When hope has almost fled, at the hour of sor-
    est need,
Is heard the clatter of iron hoofs and the neigh of a cours-
    ing steed.

Now let the martial music breathe its most inspiring notes,
As bursts the shout of welcome from the faltering veterans'
    throats !

What spell so much could nerve them in that losing battle's
    shock,
" Courage, boys ! It is the General ! Onward comrades ! On
    with Brock ! "

Now forward to the battery ! They lend a ready ear ;
There's a hero's form to lead them and a hero's voice to
    cheer.

And o'er the level plain they press, and up the sloping hill,
'Mid hiss of shot and volleys' smoke his cry is " Onward ! "
    still.

And now they pass the low ravine, they clamber o'er the
    wall ;
The fatal death-shot strikes him ; they see their leader fall.

" Push on, push on, York volunteers ! " brave words—they
    were his last,
And like the vision of a dream the charging column passed.

He heard their cry of vengeance as they reached the moun-
    tain's crest,
Then rushed in purpling tide the flood of life-blood from his
    breast.

You've read the rest ; their comrades came to stay their sec-
    ond flight,
Dashed on to meet the foe in blue and hurled them from
    the height.

Then, Canada, was seen thy might ! by equal ardour led,
Fought Indians like white men, and coloured men like red

One spirit moved, one thought inspired that gallant little
    band,
That foot of no invading foe should e'er pollute their land.

A thousand men laid down their arms to force inferior far ;
Blush, fickle land of commerce, for thy myrmidons of war.

Sleep, heroes ! Rest upon the hill where valor's deed was
    done,
No flower shall ever wither in a crown so nobly won.

While Canada can rear her sons, the bravest of the brave,
From the tempests of Atlantic to the placid western wave,

So surely as shall come the day that tells your deathless fame,
Shall future patriots mourn you and festal rites proclaim.

And thou, whose sacred dust entombed on yonder summit
    lies,
Beneath that noble monument far-reaching toward the skies,

Thy name shall be a holy word, a trumpet-note to all,
When bravery's arm is needed and they hear their country's
    call.

And future sires shall take their sons at evening on their
    knee,
And tell the old tale over, and thus shall speak of thee —

" His is the noblest name we have in all our bright array ;
He taught our youth to falter not tho' death might bar the
    way ;

" He showed our might, he led our arms, he conquered,
    tho' he fell ;
He gave up all he had—his life—for the land he loved so
    well."

BROTHERS AWAKE!

BY AIMEE HUNTINGDON, PICTOU, N. S.

BROTHERS awake! There are traitors around us,
Seeking their country and ours to betray;
Striving to sever the links that have bound us
To dear Mother England for many a day.

List to their pitiful, cowardly croaking,
Bidding us barter our heritage grand;
Bend, like dumb cattle, our necks to the yoking,
Yield unto strangers our glorious land.

Surely too long we have borne with their scheming;
Now let them learn that forbearance is o'er!
Teach them that Canada's sons are not dreaming;
Brothers awaken! and slumber no more.

Say, shall not we, whom our country has nourished,
Fight for her weal 'gainst the treacherous crew?
Shall it be said that foul treason has flourished
'Neath the proud folds of the Red, White and Blue.

Never! With courage undimmed and undaunted,
Crush, ere it blossoms, the seed they have sown;
Back in their teeth fling the boasts they have flaunted,
Pause not, nor rest, till the day be our own.

Croakers and cravens and patriot-haters,
Soon shall their schemes in the dust be laid low;
Then shall this land of ours, freed from the traitors,
To her bright destiny joyfully go.

DESTINY.

BY T. E. MOBERLY.

Awake ! awake ! old England,
 Rise from thine island lair ;
The sun of empire dawning,
 Gleams on thy dew-wet hair.

Outstretch thy limbs majestic !
 Peal out thy thund'rous roar !
Thy lion brood will greet thee
 From every sea and shore.

Temptations now beset them,
 Foes from behind, before ;
Her children look to England,
 They wait the lion's roar—

The royal invitation
 To the lion brood afar,
To share the royal burden,
 Be it in peace or war.

To share the royal honour,
 Bright guerdon of the day ! ·
When England and her offspring
 Shall join in equal sway.

Awake ! awake ! old England
 Rise from thine island lair.
Thy lion brood are longing
 Thy destiny to share.

MY OWN CANADIAN HOME.

BY E. G. NELSON.

THOUGH other skies may be as bright,
　And other lands as fair ;
Though charms of other climes invite
　My wandering footsteps there,
Yet there is one, the peer of all
　Beneath bright heaven's dome ;
Of thee I sing, O happy land,
　My own Canadian home !

Thy lakes and rivers, as "the voice
　Of many waters," raise
To Him who planned their vast extent,
　A symphony of praise.
Thy mountain peaks o'erlook the clouds—
　They pierce the azure skies ;
They bid thy sons be strong and true—
　To great achievements rise.

A noble heritage is thine,
　So grand, and fair, and free ;
A fertile land, where he who toils
　Shall well rewarded be.
And he who joys in nature's charms,
　Exulting, here may view—
Scenes of enchantment—strangely fair,
　Sublime in form and hue.

Shall not the race that tread thy plains
　Spurn all that would enslave ?
Or they who battle with thy tides,
　Shall not that race be brave ?
Shall not Niagara's mighty voice
　Inspire to actions high ?
'Twere easy such a land to love,
　Or for her glory die.

And doubt not should a foeman's hand
    Be armed to strike at thee,
Thy trumpet call throughout the land
    Need scarce repeated be !
As bravely as on Queenston's Heights,
    Or as in Lundy's Lane.
Thy sons will battle for thy rights,
    And freedom's cause maintain.

Did kindly heaven afford to me
    The choice where I would dwell,
Fair Canada ! that choice should be,
    The land I love so well.
I love thy hills and valleys wide,
    Thy waters' flash and foam ;
May God in love o'er thee preside,
    My own Canadian home !

IN MEMORY OF WILLIAM A. FOSTER.

BY CHARLES MAIR.

AND he is gone who led the few
    Forecasters of a nation fair :
That gentle spirit strong and true,
    As ever breathed Canadian air !

Forever fled ! the kindly face,
    The eager look, the lambent eye,
Still haunted by a boyish grace—
    Can these from recollection fly ?

The counsel sound, the judgment clear,
    The mild thought brooding over all ;
The ready smile, the ready tear—
    Can these from recollection fall ?

Ah ! well do I remember still
　The sultry day, whose sun had set ;
The hostel near the tower-crowned hill,
　The parlour dim where first we met ;

The flush of joy, when o'er the wine,
　On that pale eve of loftier times,
He put his friendly hand in mine,
　And praised my poor Canadian rhymes ;

And sung the old Canadian songs,
　And played the old Canadian airs,
Then turned his smile on fancied wrongs,
　And laughed away a youth's despairs ;

And said : " Throw sickly thoughts aside—
　Let's build on native fields our fame ;
Nor seek to blend our patriot pride
　With alien greed or alien shame !

" Nor trust the falterers who despond—
　The doubting spirits which divine
No stable future save beyond
　Their long, imaginary line !

" But mark, by fate's strong finger traced,
　Our country's rise ; see time unfold,
In our own land a nation based
　On manly worth, not lust of gold.

" Its bourne, the home of generous life,
　Of ample freedom, slowly won,
Of modest maid and faithful wife,
　Of simple love 'twixt sire and son.

" Nor lessened would the duty be
　To rally, then, around the throne,

A filial nation, strong and free—
Great Britain's child to manhood grown !

" But lift the curtain which deceives,
The veil that intercepts the sight,
The drapery dependence weaves
To screen us from the nobler light.

" First feel throughout the throbbing land
A nation's pulse, a nation's pride,
The independent life—then stand
Erect, unbound, at Britain's side !"

And many a year has fled, and now
The tongue which voiced the thought is stilled ;
The veil yet hangs o'er many a brow,
The glorious dream is unfulfilled.

Yet ocean unto ocean cries !
For us their mighty tides go forth.
We front the sun—behind us lies
The mystery of the unconquered North !

And ardent Aspiration peers
Beyond the clouds, beyond the night,
Beyond the faltering, paltering years,
And there beholds the Breaking Light.

For though the thoughtful mind has passed
From mortal ken, the generous hand—
The seed they sowed has sprung at last,
And grows and blossoms through the land.

And time will realize the dream,
The light yet spread o'er land and wave ;
And Honour, in that hour supreme,
Will hang his wreath o'er Foster's grave.

A BALLAD FOR BRAVE WOMEN.

BY CHARLES MAIR.

A STORY worth telling, our annals afford,
'Tis the wonderful journey of Laura Secord!
Her poor crippled spouse hobbled home
        With the news
That Bœrstler was nigh! " Not a minute to lose,
Not an instant," said Laura, " for stoppage or pause—
I must hurry and warn our brave troops at Decaws."
" What! you!" said her husband "to famish and tire!"
" Yes, me!" said brave Laura, her bosom on fire.
" And how will you pass the gruff sentry?" said he,
" Who is posted so near us?"

               " Just wait till you see;
The foe is approaching, and means to surprise
Our troops, as you tell me. Oh, husband, there flies
No dove with a message so needful as this—
I'll take it, I'll bear it, good bye, with a kiss."
Then a biscuit she ate, tucked her skirts well about,
And a bucket she slung on each arm, and went out

'Twas the bright blush of dawn, when the stars melt from
    sight,
Dissolved by its breath like a dream of the night;
When heaven seems opening on man and his pain,
Ere the rude day strengthens, and shuts it again.
But Laura had eyes for her duty alone—
She marked not the glow and the gloom that were thrown
By the nurslings of morn, by the cloud-lands at rest,
By the spells of the East, and the weirds of the West.

Behind was the foe, full of craft and of guile ;
Before her, a long day of travel and toil.
"No time this for gazing," said Laura, as near
To the sentry she drew.

     "Halt ! you cannot pass here."
"I cannot pass here! Why, sirrah, you drowse,
Are you blind? Don't you see I am off to my cows."
"Well, well you can go." So she wended her way
To the pasture's lone side, where the farthest cow lay,
Got her up, caught a teat, and with pail at her knees,
Made her budge, inch by inch. till she drew by degrees
To the edge of the fore-t. "I've hoaxed, on my word,
Both you and the sentry," said Laura Secord.

With a lingering look at her home, then away
She sped through the wild wood—a wilderness gray—
Nature's privacy, haunt of a virgin sublime
And the mother who bore her. as ancient as Time ;
Where the linden had space for its fans and its flowers,
The balsam its tents, and the cedar its bowers ;
Where the lord of the forest, the oak, had its realm,
The ash its domain, and its kingdom the elm ;
Where the pine bowed its antlers in tempests, and gave
To the ocean of leaves the wild dash of the wave,
And the mystical hemlock—The forest's high-priest—
Hung its weird, raking, top-gallant branch to the east.

And denser and deeper the solitude grew,
The underwood thickened. and drenched her with dew ;
She tripped over moss-covered logs, fell, arose,
Sped, and stumbled again by the hour, till her clothes
Were rent by the branches and thorns, and her feet
Grew tender and way-worn and blistered with heat.
And on, ever on, through the forest she passed,
Her soul in her task, but each pulse beating fast,

For shadowy forms seemed to flit from the glades
And beckon her into their limitless shades :
And mystical sounds—in the forest alone,
Ah ! who has not heard them ?—the voices, the moan,
Or the sigh of mute nature, which sinks on the ear,
And fills us with sadness or thrills us with fear?
And who, lone and lost, in the wilderness deep,
Has not felt the strange fancies, the tremors which creep,
And assemble within, till the heart 'gins to fail,
The courage to flinch, and the cheeks to grow pale,
'Midst the shadows which mantle the spirit that broods
In the sombre, the deep haunted heart of the woods?

She stopped—it was noonday. The wilds she espied
Seemed solitudes numberless. " Help me ! " she cried ;
Her piteous lips parched with thirst, and her eyes
Strained with gazing. The sun in his infinite skies
Looked down on no creature more hapless than she,
For woman is woman where'er she may be.
For a moment she faltered, then came to her side
The heroine's spirit—the Angel of Pride.
One moment she faltered. Beware ! What is this?
The coil of the serpent ! the rattlesnake's hiss !
One moment, then onward. What sounds far and near?
The howl of the wolf, yet she turned not in fear
Nor bent from her course, till her eye caught a gleam
From the woods of a meadow through which flowed a stream,
Pure and sweet with the savour of leaf and of flower.
By the night dew distilled, and the soft forest shower ;
Pure and cold as its spring in the rock crystalline,
Whence it gurgled and gushed 'twixt the roots of the pine.

And blessed above bliss is the pleasure of thirst,
Where there's water to quench it ; for pleasure is nursed
In the cradle of pain, and twin marvels are they
Whose inter-dependence is born with our clay.
Yes, blessed is water, and blessed is thirst,

Where there's water to quench it ; but this is the worst
Of this life, that we reck not the blessings God sends,
Till denied them.   But Laura, who felt she had friends
In heaven as well as on earth, knew to thank
The giver of all things, and gratefully drank.

Once more on the pathway, through swamp and through
      mire,
Through covert and thicket, through bramble and 'brier,
She toiled to the highway, then over the hill,
And down the deep valley, and past the new mill,
And through the next woods, till, at sunset, she came
To the first British picket and murmured her name ;
Thence, guarded by Indians, footsore and pale
She was led to Fitzgibbon, and told him her tale.

For a moment her reason forsook her ; she raved,
She laughed, and she cried—" They are saved, they are
      saved !"
Then her senses returned, and with thanks loud and deep
Sounding sweetly around her she sank into sleep.
And Bœrstler came up, but his movements were known,
His force was surrounded, his scheme was o'erthrown
By a woman's devotion—on stone be't engraved—
The foeman was beaten and Burlington saved.

Ah ! faithful to death were our women of yore !
Have they fled with the past to be heard of no more ?
No, no !   Though this laurelled one sleeps in the grave,
We have maidens as true, we have matrons as brave ;
And should Canada ever be forced to the test—
To spend for our country the blood of her best !
When her sons lift the linstock and brandish the sword,
Her daughters will think of brave Laura Secord !

THE UNITED EMPIRE LOYALISTS.

BY THE REV. LE ROY HOOKER

In the brave old Revolution days,
So by our sires 'tis told,
King's-men and Rebels, all ablaze
With wrath and wrong,
Strove hard and long :
And, fearsome to behold,
O'er town and wilderness afar,
O'er quaking land and sea and air,
All dark and stern the cloud of war
· In bursting thunder rolled.

Men of one blood—of British blood,
Rushed to the mortal strife ;
Men brothers born,
In hate and scorn·
Shed each the other's life.
Which had the right and which the wrong
It boots not now to say ;
But when at last
The war-cloud passed,
Cornwallis sailed away ;
He sailed away, and left the field
To those who knew right well to wield
The powers of war, but not to yield,
Though Britons fought the day.

Cornwallis sailed away, but left
Full many a loyal man,
Who wore the red,
And fought and bled
Till Royal George's banner fled
Not to return again.

What did they then, those loyal men,
  When Britain's cause was lost?
    Did they consent,
    And dwell content
Where Crown, and Law and Parliament
  Were trampled in the dust?

Dear were the homes where they were born;
  Where slept their honored dead;
    And rich and wide
    On every side
Their fruitful acres spread;
But dearer to their faithful hearts
  Than home, or gold, or lands,
Were Britain's laws, and Britain's crown,
And Britain's flag of long renown,
  And grip of British hands.

They would not spurn the glorious old,
  To grasp the gaudy new;
Of yesterday's rebellion born,
They held the upstart power in scorn—
  To Britain they stood true,

With high resolve they looked their last
  On home and native land;
    And sore they wept
    O'er those that slept
In honored graves that must be kept
  By grace of stranger's hand.

They looked their last, and got them out
  Into the wilderness,
  The stern old wilderness,
    All dark and rude
    And unsubdued;
  The savage wilderness,

Where wild beasts howled,
And Indians prowled ;
The lonely wilderness,
Where social joys must be forgot,
And budding childhood grow untaught ;
Where hopeless hunger might assail
Should autumn's promised fruitage fail ;
Where sickness, unrestrained by skill,
Might slay their dear ones at its will ;
Where they must lay
Their dead away,
Without the man of God to say
The sad sweet words, how dear to men,
Of resurrection hope !   But then
'Twas British wilderness !
Where they might sing,
God save the King !
And live protected by his laws,
And loyally uphold his cause !
'Twas welcome wilderness !
Though dark and rude
And unsubdued ;
Though wild beasts howled
And Indians prowled ;
For there their sturdy hands,
By hated treasons undefiled,
Might win from the Canadian wild
A home on British lands !

These be thy heroes, Canada !
These men of proof, whose test
Was in the fevered pulse of strife
When foeman thrusts at foeman's life ;
And in that stern behest,
When right must toil for scanty bread,
While wrong on sumptuous fare is fed,
And men must choose between !

When right must shelter 'neath the skies,
While wrong in lordly mansion lies,
    And men must choose between !
When right is cursed and crucified,
While wrong is cheered and glorified,
    And men must choose between !

    Stern was the test,
    And sorely pressed,
That proved their blood best of the best.
And when for Canada you pray,
    Implore kind Heaven
    That, like a leaven,
The hero-blood which then was given
May quicken in her veins alway :—
That from those worthy sires may spring,
    In number as the stars,
Strong-hearted sons, whose glorying
    Shall be in Right,
    Though recreant Might
Be strong against her in the fight,
    And many be her scars !
So, like the sun, her honored name
Shall shine to latest years the same.

THE CAPTURE OF DETROIT,
1812

Being part of Act IV. of Charles Mair's Drama of
TECUMSEH.

———•◆•———

ACT IV.

Enter CHORUS.

War is declared, unnatural and wild,
By Revolution's calculating sons !
So leave the home of mercenary minds,
And wing with me, in your uplifted thoughts,
Away to our unyielding Canada !
There to behold the Genius of the Land,
Beneath her singing pine and sugared tree,
Companioned with the lion, Loyalty.

SCENE FIRST.—A ROOM IN FORT GEORGE.

Enter GENERAL BROCK *reading a despatch from Montreal.*

BROCK. Prudent and politic Sir George Prevost !
Hull's threatened ravage of our western coast,
Hath more breviloquence than your despatch.
Storms are not stilled by reasoning with air,
Nor fires quenched by a syrup of sweet words.
So to the wars, Diplomacy, for now
Our trust is in our arms and arguments
Delivered only from the cannon's mouth !

[*Rings.*

Enter an ORDERLY.

ORDERLY. Your Exc'llency ?
BROCK.   Bid Colonel Proctor come !

[*Exit Orderly.*

Now might the head of gray Experience
Shake o'er the problems that surround us here.
I am no stranger to the brunt of war,
But all the odds so lean against our side
That valor's self might tremble for the issue.
Could England stretch its full, assisting hand
Then might I smile though velvet-footed time
Struck all his claws at once into our flesh ;
But England, noble England, fights for life,
Couching the knightly lance for liberty
'Gainst a new dragon that affrights the world.
And, now, how many noisome elements
Would plant their greed athwart this country's good !
How many demagogues bewray its cause !
How many aliens urge it to surrender !
Our present good must match their present ill.
And, on our frontiers, boldest deeds in war,
Dismay the foe, and strip the loins of faction.

Enter COLONEL PROCTOR.

Time waits not for conveniency ; I trust
Your preparations have no further needs
    PROCTOR.　All is in readiness, and I can leave
For Amherstburgh at once.
    BROCK.　　　　　　　　Then tarry not,
For time is precious to us now as powder.
You understand my wishes and commands ?
    PROCTOR.　I know them and shall match them with
      obedience.
    BROCK.　Rest not within the limit of instructions
If you can better them, for they should bind
The feeble only ; able men enlarge
And shape them to their needs.　Much must be done
That lies in your discretion.　At Detroit
Hull vaunts his strength, and meditates invasion,
And loyalty, unarmed, defenceless, bare,
May let this boaster light upon our shores
Without one manly motion of resistance.

So whilst I open Parliament at York,
Close it again, and knit our volunteers,
Be yours the task to head invasion off.
Act boldly, but discreetly, and so draw
Our interest to the balance, that affairs
May hang in something like an even scale,
Till I can join you with a fitting force,
And batter this old Hull until he sinks.
So fare-you-well—success attend your mission !

    PROCTOR.   Farewell, sir !   I shall do my best in this,
And put my judgment to a prudent use
In furtherance of all.

                                 [*Exit* PROCTOR.

    BROCK. Prudent he will be—'tis a vice in him.
For in the qualities of every mind
There's one o'ergrows, and prudence in this man
Tops all the rest. 'Twill suit our present needs.
But, boldness, go with me ! for, if I know
My nature well, I shall do something soon
Whose consequence will make the nation cheer,
Or hiss me to my grave.

              Re-enter ORDERLY.

    ORDERLY.   Your Exc'llency,
Some settlers wait without.

    BROCK. Whence do they come ?

          Enter COLONEL MACDONELL.

    ORDERLY. From the raw clearings up Lake Erie, Sir.

    BROCK. Go bring them here at once. (*Exit* ORDERLY.)
    The very men
Who meanly shirk their service to the crown !
A breach of duty to be remedied,
For disaffection like an ulcer spreads
Until the caustic ointment of the law,
Sternly applied, eats up and stays corruption.

    (*Enter* DEPUTATION OF YANKEE SETTLERS.)

Good morrow, worthy friends ; I trust you bear
Good hopes in loyal hearts for Canada.

1ST SETTLER. That kind o' crop's a failure in our county.
Gen'ral, we came to talk about this war
With the United States. It ain't quite fair
To call out settlers from the other side.
    BROCK. From it yet on it too ! Why came you thence ?
Is land so scarce in the United States ?
Are there no empty townships, wilds or wastes
In all their borders but you must encroach
On ours ?   And, being here, how dare you make
Your dwelling-places harbours of sedition
And furrow British soil with alien ploughs
To feed our enemies ?   There is not scope,
Not room enough in all this wilderness
For men so base.
    2ND SETTLER. Why, General, we thought
You wanted settlers here.
    BROCK.   Settlers indeed !
But with the soldier's courage to defend
The land of their adoption.   This attack
On Canada is foul and unprovoked ;
The hearts are vile, the hands are traitorous
That will not help to hurl invasion back.
Beware the lariat of the law !   'Tis thrown
With aim so true in Canada it brings
Sedition to the ground at every cast.
    1ST SETTLER. Well, General, we're not your British sort,
But if we were we know that Canada
Is naught compared with the United States
We have no faith in her, but much in them.
    BROCK. You have no faith !   Then take a creed from me !
For I believe in Britain's Empire, and
In Canada. its true and loyal son.
Who yet shall rise to greatness, and shall stand
At England's shoulder helping her to guard
True liberty throughout a faithless world.
Here is a creed for arsenals and camps,
For hearts and heads that seek their country's good ;
So, go at once, and meditate on it !

I have no time to parley with you now—
But think on this as well ! that traitors, spies,
And aliens who refuse to take up arms,
Forfeit their holdings, and must leave this land,
Or dangle nearer heaven than they wish.
So to your homes, and ponder your condition.

[Exeunt Settlers ruefully.

This foreign element will hamper us.
Its alien spirit ever longs for change,
And union with the States.

MACDONELL. O fear it not,
Nor magnify the girth of noisy men !
Their name is faction, and their numbers few.
While everywhere encompassing them stands
The silent element that doth not change ;
That points with steady finger to the Crown—
True as the needle to the viewless pole,
And stable as its star !

BROCK. I know it well,
And trust to it alone for earnestness,
Accordant counsels, loyalty and faith.
But give me these—and let the Yankees come !
With our poor handful of inhabitants,
We can defend our forest wilderness,
And spurn the bold invader from our shores.

Re-enter ORDERLY.

ORDERLY. Your boat is ready, sir !
BROCK. Man it at once—
I shall forthwith to York.

[Exeunt.

SCENE SECOND.—YORK, THE CAPITAL OF UPPER
CANADA. THE SPACE IN FRONT OF OLD
GOVERNMENT HOUSE.

Enter two U. E. LOYALISTS, *separately.*

1ST U. E. LOYALIST. Well met, my friend ! A stirrer
like myself.

2ND U. E. LOYALIST.   Yes, affairs make me so.   Such
    stirring times
Since Brock returned and opened Parliament !
Read you his speech ?
    1ST U. E. LOYALIST.   That from the Throne ?
    2ND U. E. LOYALIST.   Ay, that !
    1ST U. E. LOYALIST.   You need not ask, since 'tis on
    every tongue,
Unstaled by repetition.   I affirm
Words never showered upon more fruitful soil
To nourish valor's growth.
    2ND U. E. LOYALIST.   That final phrase—
Oh it struck home : a sentence to be framed
And hung in every honorable heart
For daily meditation.
" We are engaged in an awful and eventful contest.   By
unanimity and dispatch in our councils, and by vigour in our
operations, we may teach the enemy this lesson, that a country
defended by free men, enthusiastically devoted to the cause of
their king and constitution, can never be conquered."
    1ST U. E. LOYALIST.   That reaches far ; a text to fortify
Imperial doctrine and Canadian rights.
Sedition skulks, and feels its blood a cold,
Since first it fell upon the public ear.
    2ND U. E. LOYALIST.   There is a magic in this soldier's
    tongue.
O language is a common instrument ;
But when a master touches it—what sounds !
    1ST U. E. LOYALIST.   What sounds indeed !   But Brock
    can use his sword
Still better than his tongue.   Our state affairs,
Conned and digested by his eager mind
Draw into form, and even now his voice
Cries, Forward !   To the front !
    2nd U. E. LOYALIST.   Look—here he comes !
    1ST U. E. LOYALIST.   There's matter in the wind ; let's
    draw a-near.

Enter GENERAL BROCK, *accompanied by* MACDONELL,
NICHOL, ROBINSON *and other Canadian Officers
and friends conversing.*

BROCK   'Tis true our Province faces heavy odds ;
Of regulars but fifteen hundred men
To guard a frontier of a thousand miles ;
Of volunteers what aidance we can draw
From seventy thousand widely scattered souls.
A meagre showing 'gainst the enemy's
If numbers be the test.   But odds lie not
In numbers only, but in spirit too—
Witness the might of England's little isle !
And what made England great will keep her so—
The free soul and the valour of her sons ;
And what exalts her will sustain you now
If you contain her courage and her faith.
So not the odds so much are to be feared
As private disaffection, treachery—
Those openers of the door to enemies—
And the poor crouching spirit that gives way
Ere it is forced to yield.
    ROBINSON.   No fear of that !
    BROCK. I trust there is not ; yet I speak of it
As what is to be feared more than the odds.
For like to forests are communities—
Fair at a distance, entering you find
The rubbish and the underbrush of states,
'Tis ever the mean soul that counts the odds,
And, where you find this spirit, pluck it up—
'Tis full of mischief.
    MACDONELL.   It is almost dead.
England's vast war, our weakness, and the eagle
Whetting his beak at Sandwich, with one claw
Already in our side, put thought to steep
In cold conjecture for a time, and gave
A text to alien tongues.   But, since you came,
Depression turns to smiling, and men see

That dangers well opposed may be subdued
Which shunned would overwhelm us.
    BROCK.   Hold to this !
For since the storm has struck us we must face it.
What is our present count of volunteers ?
    NICHOL. More than you called for have assembled, Sir—
The flower of York and Lincoln.
    BROCK.   Some will go
To guard our frontier at Niagara.
Which must be strengthened even at the cost
Of York itself. The rest to the Detroit,
Where, with Tecumseh's force, our regulars,
And Kent and Essex loyal volunteers,
We'll give this Hull a taste of steel so cold
His teeth will chatter at it, and his scheme
Of easy conquest vanish into air.

(Enter a COMPANY *of* MILITIA *with their* OFFICERS, *unarm-*
ed. They salute, march across the stage, and make their
exit.)

What men are those ? Their faces are familiar.
    ROBINSON. Some farmers whom you furloughed at Fort
        George,
To tend their fields, which still they leave half-reaped
To meet invasion.
    BROCK.   I remember it !
The jarring needs of harvest-time and war,
'Twixt whose necessities grave hazards lay.
    ROBINSON. They only thought to save their children's
        bread,
And then return to battle with light hearts.
For, though their hard necessities o'erpoised
Their duty for the moment, these are men
Who draw their pith from loyal roots, their sires,
Dug up by revolution, and cast out
To hovel in the bitter wilderness,
And wring, with many a tussle, from the wolf
Those very fields which cry for harvesters.

BROCK. O, I observed them closely at Fort George—
Red-hot for action in their summer sleeves,
And others drilling in their naked feet—
Our poor equipment (which disgraced us there) ·.
Too scanty to go round. See they get arms,
An ample outfit and good quarters, too.
  NICHOL. They shall be well provided for in all.

Enter COLONELS BABY* *and* ELLIOTT.

BROCK. Good morning both; what news from home,
    Baby ?
  BABY. None, none your Exc'llency—whereat we fear this
Hull is in our rear at Amherstburg.
  BROCK. Not yet ; what I unsealed last night reports
Tecumseh to have foiled the enemy
In two encounters at the Canard bridge.
A noble fellow as I hear, humane,
Lofty and bold, and rooted in our cause.
  BABY. I know him well ; a chief of matchless force.
If Mackinaw should fall—that triple key
To inland seas and teeming wilderness—
The bravest in the west will flock to him.
  BROCK. 'Twere well he had an inkling of affairs.
My letters say he chafes at my delay,
Not mine, but thine, thou dull and fatuous House—
Which, in a period that whips delay,
When men should spur themselves and flash in action,
Let'st idly leak the unpurchasable hours
From our scant measure of most precious time !
  BABY. 'Tis true, Your Exc'llency, some cankered minds
Have been a daily hind'rance in our House.
No measure so essential, bill so fair
But they would foul it by some cunning clause,
Wrenching the needed statute from its aim
By sly injection of their false opinion.
But this you cannot charge to us whose hearts
Are faithful to our trust ; nor yet delay ;

---

*Pronounced Baw-bée,

For, Exc'llency, you hurry on so fast
That other men wheeze after, out of breath,
And haste itself, disparaged, lags behind.
.   BROCK. Friends, pardon me, you stand not in reproof.
But haste, the evil of the age in peace,
Is war's auxiliary, confederate
With time himself in urgent great affairs.
So must we match it with the flying hours !
I shall prorogue this tardy Parliament,
And promptly head our forces for Detroit.
Meanwhile, I wish you, in advance of us,
To speed unto your homes.   Spread everywhere
Throughout the West, broad tidings of our coming.
Which, by the counter currents of reaction,
Will tell against our foes and for our friends.
As for the rest, such loyal men as you
Need not our counsel ; so, good journey both !
    BABY. We shall not spare our transport or ourselves.

Enter a travel-stained MESSENGER.

ELLIOTT. Good-bye.
BABY.   Tarry a moment, Elliott !
Here comes a messenger—let's have his news.
    MESSENGER. It is his Excellency whom I seek.
I come, sir, with despatches from the west.
    BROCK. Tidings I trust to strengthen all our hopes.
    MESSENGER. News of grave interest, this not the worst.
                [Handing a letter to GENERAL BROCK.
BROCK. No, by my soul, for Mackinaw is ours !
That vaunted fort, whose gallant capture frees
Our red allies.   This is important news !
What of Detroit ?
    MESSENGER.   Things vary little there.
Hull's soldiers scour our helpless settlements,
Our aliens join them, but the loyal mass —
Sullen, yet overawed, longs for relief.
    BROCK. I hope to better this anon.   You, sirs,
                      [To his aides.

Come with me ; here is matter to dispatch
At once to Montreal.   Farewell, my friends.

[*To Baby and Elliott.*

BABY.   We feel now what will follow this, farewell !

[*Exeunt* BABY, ELLIOTT *and* MESSENGER.

BROCK.   Now, gentlemen, prepare against our needs,
That no neglect may check us at the start,
Or mar our swift advance.   And, for our cause,
As we believe it just in sight of God,
So should it triumph in the sight of man,
Whose generous temper, at the first, assigns
Right to the weaker side, yet coldly draws
Damning conclusions from its failure.   Now
Betake you to your tasks with double zeal ;
And, meanwhile, let our joyful tidings spread !

[*Exeunt.*

SCENE THIRD.—THE SAME.

Enter two OLD MEN *of York, severally.*

1ST OLD MAN.   Good morrow, friend ! a fair and fitting
time
To take our airing, and to say farewell.
'Tis here, I think, we bid our friends God-speed,
A waftage, peradventure, to their graves.
2ND OLD MAN.   'Tis a good cause they die for, if they
fall.
By this grey pate, if I were young again,
I would no better journey.   Young again !
This hubbub sets old pulses on the bound
As I were in my teens.

Enter a CITIZEN.

What news afoot ?
CITIZEN.   Why everyone's afoot and coming here.
York's citizens are turned to warriors ;
The learned professions go a-soldiering,

And gentle hearts beat high for Canada !
For, as you pass, on every hand you see,
Through the neglected openings of each house—
Through doorways, windows—our Canadian maids
Strained by their parting lovers to their breasts ;
And loyal matrons busy round their lords,
Buckling their arms on, or, with tearful eyes,
Kissing them to the war !

1st OLD MAN. The volunteers
Will pass this way?

CITIZEN. Yes, to the beach, and there
Embark for Burlington, whence they will march
To Long Point, taking open boats again,
To plough the shallow Erie's treacherous flood.
Such leaky craft as farmers market with :
Rare bottoms, one sou-wester-driven wave
Would heave against Lake Erie's wall of shore,
And dash to fragments. 'Tis an awful hazard—
A danger which in apprehension lies,
Yet palpable unto the spirit's touch,
As earth to finger.

1st OLD MAN. Let us hope a calm
May lull this fretful and ill-tempered lake
Whilst they ascend.

[*Military music is heard.*

CITIZEN. Hark ! here our soldiers come.

Enter GENERAL BROCK, *with his aides,* MACDONELL and
GLEGG, NICHOL, *and other officers, followed by the Volunteers in companies. A concourse of citizens.*

MACDONELL. Our fellows show the mark of training, sir,
And many, well in hand, yet full of fire,
Are burning for distinction.

BROCK. This is good :
Love of distinction is the fruitful soil
From which brave actions spring ; and superposed
On love of country, these strike deeper root,

And grow to greater greatness, Cry a halt—
A word here—then away !

> [*Flourish. The Volunteers halt, form line,*
> *and order arms.*

Ye men of Canada !
Subjects with me of that Imperial Power
Whose liberties are marching round the earth :
I need not urge you now to follow me,
Though what befalls will try your stubborn faith
In the fierce fire and crucible of war.
I need not urge you, who have heard the voice
Of loyalty, and answered to its call.
Who has not read the insults of the foe—
The manifesto of his purposed crimes ?
That foe, whose poison-plant, false liberty,
Runs o'er his body politic and kills
Whilst seeming to adorn it, fronts us now !
Threats our poor Province to annihilate,
And should he find the red men by our side —
Poor injured souls, who but defend their own—
Calls black Extermination from its hell,
To stalk abroad, and stench your land with slaughter.
These are our weighty arguments for war,
Wherein armed Justice will enclasp its sword,
And sheath it in its bitter adversary ;
Wherein we'll turn our bayonet-points to pens,
And write in blood :—*Here lies the poor invader ;*
Or be ourselves struck down by hailing death :
Made stepping stones for foes to walk upon—
The lifeless gangways to our country's ruin.
For now we look not with the eye of fear ;
We reck not if this strange mechanic frame—
Stop in an instant in the shock of war.
Our death may build into our country's life,
And failing this, 'twere better still to die
Than live the breathing spoils of infamy.
Then forward for our cause and Canada !

Forward for Britain's Empire—peerless arch
Of Freedom's raising, whose majestic span
Is axis to the world ! On, on, my friends !
The task our country sets must we perform —
Wring peace from war, or perish in its storm !

[*Excitement and leave-taking. The volunteers
break into column and sing :*

O hark to the voice from the lips of the free !
O hark to the cry from the lakes to the sea !
Arm ! arm ! the invader is wasting our coasts,
And tainting the air of our land with his hosts.
Arise ! then, arise ! let us rally and form,
And rush like the torrent, and sweep like the storm,
On the foes of our King, of our country adored,
Of the flag that was lost, but in exile restored !

Aud whose was the flag ? and whose was the soil?
And whose was the exile, the suffering, the toil ?
Our Fathers' ! who carved in the forest a name,
And left us rich heirs of their freedom and fame.
Oh, dear to our hearts is that flag, and the land
Our Fathers bequeathed—'tis the work of their hand !
And the soil they redeemed from the woods with renown
The might of their sons will defend for the Crown !

Our hearts they are one, and our hands they are free,
From clime unto clime, and from sea unto sea !
And chaos will come to the States that annoy,
But our Empire united what foe can destroy ?
Then away ! to the front ! march ! comrades away !
In the lists of each hour crowd the work of a day !
We will follow our leader to the fields far and nigh,
And for Canada fight, and for Canada die !

[*Exeunt with military music.*

SCENE FOURTH.—Fort Detroit.—The American Camp.

Enter General Hull, Colonel Cass *and other Officers.*

Cass. Come, General, we must insist on reasons !
Your order to withdraw from Canada
Will blow to mutiny, and put to shame
That proclamation which I wrote for you,
Wherein 'tis proudly said, " *We are prepared
To look down opposition, our strong force*

But vanguard of a mightier still to come ! "
And men have been attracted to our cause
Who now will curse us for this breach of faith.
Consider, sir, again !
    HULL.   I am not bound
To tack my reasons to my orders ; this
Is my full warrant and authority—

                [*Pointing to his Instructions.*

Yet, I have ample grounds for what I do.
    CASS.   What are they, then ?
    HULL.   First, that this proclamation
Meets not with due response, wins to our side
The thief and refugee, not honest men.
These plainly rally round their government.
    1ST OFFICER.   Why, yes ; there's something lacking in
        this people,
If we must conquer them to set them free.
    HULL.   Ay, and our large force must be larger still,
If we would change these Provinces to States.
Then, Colonel Proctor's intercepted letter—
Bidding the captor of Fort Mackinaw
Send but five thousand warriors from the West,
Which, be it artifice or not, yet points
To great and serious danger.   Add to this
Brock's rumoured coming with his Volunteers,
All burning to avenge their fathers' wrongs,
And our great foe, Tecumseh, fired o'er his ;
These are the reasons ; grave enough, I think,
Which urge me to withdraw from Canada,
And wait for further force ; so go, at once,
And help our soldiers to recross the river.
    CASS.   But I see——
    HULL.   No " buts"!   You have my orders.
    CASS.   No solid reason here, naught but a group
Of flimsy apprehensions——
    HULL.   Go at once !
Who kicks at judgment, lacks it.

CASS.   I——
HULL.   No more!
I want not wrangling but obedience here.

[*Exeunt* CASS *and other officers incensed.*

Would I had ne'er accepted this command!
Old men are out of favour with the time,
And youthful folly scoffs at hoary age.
There's not a man who executes my orders
With a becoming grace; not one but sulks,
And puffs his disapproval with a frown.
And what am I?   A man whom Washington
Nodded approval of, and wrote it too!
Yet here, in judgment and discretion both,
Ripe to the dropping, scorned and ridiculed.
Oh, Jefferson, what mischief have you wrought—
Confounding Nature's order, setting fools
To prank themselves, and sit in wisdom's seat
By right divine, out-Heroding a King's!
But I shall keep straight on—pursue my course,
Responsible and with authority,
Though boasters gird at me, and braggarts frown

[*Exit.*

SCENE FIFTH.—SANDWICH, ON THE DETROIT.—A
ROOM IN THE BABY MANSION.

Enter GENERAL BROCK, COLONELS PROCTOR, GLEGG,
BABY, MACDONELL, NICHOL, ELLIOTT *and other
Officers.*

BABY. Welcome! thrice welcome!
Brave Brock, to Sandwich and this loyal roof!
Thank God, your oars, those weary levers bent
In many a wave, have been unshipped at last;
And, now, methinks those lads who stemmed the flood
Would boldly face the fire.
BROCK.   I never led
Men of more cheerful and courageous heart,

But for whose pluck, foul weather and short seas,
'Twere truth to say, had made an end of us.
Another trial will, I think, approve
The manly strain this Canada hath bred.

PROCTOR. 'Tis pity that must be denied them now,
Since all our enemies have left our shores.

BROCK. No, by my soul, it shall not be denied!
Our foe's withdrawal hath a magnet's power
And pulls my spirit clean into his fort.
But I have asked you to confer on this.
What keeps Tecumseh?

ELLIOTT.   'Tis his friend, Lefroy,
Who now rejoins him, after bootless quest
Of Iena, Tecumseh's niece.

BROCK.   Lefroy!
I had a gentle playmate of that name
In Guernsey, long ago.

BABY.   It may be he.
I know him, and, discoursing our affairs,
Have heard him speak of you, but in a strain
Peculiar to the past.

BROCK.   He had in youth
All goods belonging to the human heart,
But fell away to Revolution's side—
Impulsive ever, and o'er prompt to see
In kings but tyrants, and in laws but chains.
I have not seen or heard of him for years.

BABY. The very man!

BROCK.   'Tis strange to find him here!

ELLIOTT. He calls the red men freedom's last survival;
Says truth is only found in Nature's growth—
Her first intention, ere false knowledge rose
To frame distinctions, and exhaust the world.

BROCK. Few find like him the substance of their dreams.
But, Elliott, let us seek Tecumseh now.
Stay, friends, till we return.

                    [*Exeunt* BROCK *and* ELLIOTT.

GLEGG.   How odd to find
An old friend in this fashion !   .
    PROCTOR.   Humph ! a fool
Who dotes on forest tramps and savages.
Why, at the best, they are the worst of men ;
And this Tecumseh has so strained my temper,
So over-stept my wishes, thrid my orders,
That I would sooner ask the devil's aid
Than such as his.
    NICHOL.   Why, Brock is charmed with him !
And, as you saw, at Amherstburg he put
Most stress upon opinion when he spoke.
    MACDONELL. Already they've determined on assault.
    PROCTOR. Then most unwisely so ! There are no bounds
To this chief's rashness, and our General seems
Swayed by it too, or rashness hath a twin.
    NICHOL. Well, rashness is the wind of enterprise,
And blows its banners out.   But here they come
Who dig beneath their rashness for their reasons.

Re-enter GENERAL BROCK *and* COLONEL ELLIOTT *accompanied by* TECUMSEH, *conversing.*

    TECUMSEH. We have been much abused ! and have
        abused
Our fell destroyers, too—making our wrongs
The gauge of our revenge.   And still forced back
From the first justice and the native right,
Ever revenge hath sway.   This we would void,
And, by a common boundary, prevent.
So, granting that a portion of our own
Is still our own, then let that portion be
Confirmed by sacred treaty to our tribes.
This is my sum of asking—you have ears !
    BROCK.   Nay, then, Tecumseh, speak of it no more !
My promise is a pledge, and from a man
Who never turned his back on friend or foe.
The timely service you have done our cause,
Rating not what's to come, would warrant it.

So, if I live, possess your soul of this—
No treaty for a peace, if we prevail,
Will bear a seal that doth not guard your rights.
Here take my sash, and wear it for my sake—
Tecumseh can esteem a soldier's gift.

TECUMSEH.   Thanks, thanks, my brother, I have faith
    in you ;
My life is at your service !

BROCK.   Gentlemen,
Have you considered my proposal well
Touching the capture of Detroit by storm ?
What say you, Colonel Proctor ?

PROCTOR.   I object !
'Tis true, the enemy has left our ʳhores,
But what a sorry argument is this
For his withdrawal, which some sanguine men,
Jumping all other motives, charge to fear,
Prudence, more deeply searching, lays to craft.
Why should a foe, who far outnumbers us,
Retreat over this great river, save to lure
Our poor force after him ?   And, having crossed—
Our weakness seen, and all retreat cut off—
What would ensue but absolute surrender,
Or sheer destruction ?   'Tis too hazardous !
Discretion balks at such a mad design.

BROCK.   What say the rest ?

1ST OFFICER.   I fear 'tis indiscreet.

2ND OFFICER.   'Twould be imprudent with our scanty
    force.

BROCK.   What say you, Nichol, to my foolish scheme ?

NICHOL.   I think it feasible and prudent too.
Hull's letters, captured by Tecumseh, prove
His soldiers mutinous, himself despondent.
And dearly Rumor loves the wilderness,
Which gives a thousand echoes to a tongue
That ever swells and magnifies our strength.
And in this flux we take him, on the hinge
Of two uncertainties—his force and ours.

So, weighed, objections fall ; and our attempt,
Losing its grain of rashness, takes its rise
In clearest judgment, whose effect will nerve
All Canada to perish, ere she yield.
BROCK. My very thoughts ! what says Tecumseh now ?
   TECUMSEH. I say, attack the fort ! This very night
I'll cross my braves, if you decide on this
   BROCK. Then say no more ! Glegg, take a flag of truce,
And bear to Hull this summons to surrender.
Tell him Tecumseh and his force are here—
A host of warriors brooding on their wrongs,
Who, should resistance flush them to revenge,
Would burst from my control like wind-borne fire,
And match on earth the miseries of hell.
But, should he yield, his safety is assured.
Tell him Tecumseh's word is pledged to this,
Who, though his temperate will in peace is law,
Yet casts a loose rein to enforcèd rage.
Add what your fancy dictates ; but the stress
Place most on what I speak of—this he fears,
And these same fears, well wrought upon by you,
May prove good workers for us yet.
   GLEGG.   I go,
And shall acquit myself as best I can.
                       [*Exit* GLEGG.

   BROCK. Tecumseh, wonder not at such a message !
The guilty conscience of your foes is judge
Of their deserts, and hence 'twill be believed.
The answer may be ' nay,' so to our work—
Which perfected, we shall confer again,
Then cross at break of morn.
              [*Exeunt all but* TECUMSEH.

   TECUMSEH.   This is a man !
And our great father, waking from his sleep,
Has sent him to our aid. Master of Life,
Endue my warriors with double strength !
May the wedged helve be faithful to the axe,

The arrow fail not, and the flint be firm !
That our great vengeance, like the whirlwind fell,
May cleave, through thickets, of our enemies,
A broad path to our ravaged lands again.

[Exit.

*   *   *   *   *   *

SCENE EIGHTH.—The highway through the Forest
    leading to Fort Detroit—The Fort in the dis-
    tance ; cannon and gunners at the Gate.

Enter Tecumseh, Stayeta, *and other Chiefs and Warriors.*

    Tecumseh. There is the Long Knives' fort, within
      whose walls
We lose our lives, or find our lands to-day.
Fight for that little space—'tis wide domain !
That small enclosure shuts us from our homes.
There are the victors in the Prophet's strife—
Within that fort they lie—those bloody men
Who burnt your town, to light their triumph up,
And drove your women to the withered woods
To shudder through the cold slow-creeping night,
And help their infants to out-howl the wolf.
Oh, the base Long-Knife grows to head, not heart—
A pitiless and murdering minister
To his desires ! But let us now be strong,
And, if we conquer, merciful as strong !
Swoop like the eagles on their prey, but turn
In victory your taste to that of doves ;
For ever it has been reproach to us
That we have stained our deeds with cruelty,
And dyed our axes in our captives' blood.
So, here, retort not on a vanquished foe,
But teach him lessons in humanity.
Now let the big heart, swelling in each breast,
Strain every rib for lodgment ! Warriors !
Bend to your sacred task, and follow me.
    Stayeta. Lead on ! We follow you !

KICKAPOO CHIEF.   Advance ye braves !
TECUMSEH. Stay ! make a circuit in the open woods—
Cross, and recross, and double on the path—
So shall the Long-Knives overcount our strength.
Do this, Stayeta, whilst I meet my friend—
My brave white brother, and confer with him.

Enter GENERAL BROCK, PROCTOR, NICHOL, MACDONELL
   and other Officers and Forces, on the highway. TE-
   CUMSEH *goes down to meet them.*

BROCK. Now by God's providence we face Detroit,
Either to sleep within its walls to-night,
Or in deep beds dug by exulting foes.
Go, Nichol, make a swift reconnoissance—
We'll follow on.
       NICHOL   I shall, but, ere I go
I do entreat you, General, take the rear ;
Those guns are shrewdly placed without the gate—
One raking fire might rob us of your life,
And, this lost, all is lost.
       BROCK.   Well meant, my friend !
But I am here to lead, not follow, men
Whose confidence has come with me thus far !
Go, Nichol, to your task !

              [*Exit* NICHOL. TECUMSEH *advances.*

                    Tecumseh, hail !
Brave chieftian, you have made your promise good.
       TECUMSEH. My brother stands to his ! and I but wait
His orders to advance—my warriors
Are ripe for the assault.
       BROCK   Deploy them, then,
Upon our landward flank, and skirt the woods,
Whilst we advance in column to attack.

              [TECUMSEH *rejoins his warriors.*

Signal our batteries on the farther shore
To play upon the Fort ! Be steady friends —

Be steady ! Now upon your country turn
Your multiplying thoughts and strike for her !
Strike for your distant and inviolate homes,
Perfumed with holy prayer at this hour !
Strike ! with your fathers' virtue in your veins
You must prevail—on, on, to the attack !

[BROCK *and forces advance towards the Fort. A heavy*
cannonading from the British batteries.

Re-enter NICHOL *hastily.*

NICHOL. Stay, General ! I saw a flag of truce
Cross from the Fort to the Canadian shore.
BROCK. Halt ! There's another from yon bastion flung ;
And, see ! another waves adown the road—
Borne by an officer—what think you, Nichol ?
NICHOL. Your threats are conquerors ! The Fort is ours !
GLEGG. Yes, look ! the gunners have been all withdrawn
Who manned the cannon at yon western gate.
PROCTOR. So many men to yield without a blow !
Why, this is wonderful ! It cannot be !
BROCK. Say. rather, should not be, and yet it is !
'Tis plainly written in this captain's face.

Officer with flag of truce approaches.

OFFICER. This letter from our General contains
Proposals to capitulate—pray send
An officer to ratify the terms.

GENERAL BROCK *reads letter.*

BROCK. You have a wise and politic commander !
OFFICER. Our General, knowing your superior force—
NICHOL. (*Aside.*) O this is good ! 'tis barely half his
own !
OFFICER. And noting your demand of yesterday
With clearer judgment, doth accede to it,
To bar effusion of much precious blood
By reasonable treaty of surrender.
BROCK. Why, this is excellent, and rare discretion !

OFFICER. He fears your Indians could not be restrained.
Our women's prayers—red visions of the knife—
We know not what—have melted his stout heart,
And brought him to this pass
　　BROCK.　　　　　　　　Ay, ay, how good !
Great judgment and humanity combined.
Glegg and Macdonell go at once and sign
Those happy stipulations which restore
Fair Michigan to empire and the crown.

　　　Exeunt GLEGG, MACDONELL *and Officer with Flag.*

We shall await our officers' return—
But now prepare to occupy the Fort !
With colours flying we shall enter it,
And martial music, as befits the scene.
No Sunday ever saw a finer sight—
Three cheers for Canada and England's right !

　　　[*Shouts and congratulations from th' soldiery.*

SCENE NINTH.—FORT DETROIT.—A TUMULT OF
　　　AMERICAN SOLDIERS AND CITIZENS

Enter GENERAL HULL *and one of his officers, accompanied
　　　by* BROCK'S *Aides,* GLEGG *and* MACDONELL.

HULL.　Here is the paper !　Tell your General
Divine humanity, which hath in me
A deeper root than fear of him, thus yields :
A sheer compunction lest the savage axe
Should drink too deeply in confused revenge.
　　GLEGG.　Depend upon it, we shall tell him so,
And shall away at once.

　　　　　　　　[*Exeunt* GLEGG *and* MACDONELL.

　　HULL.　　　　　　'Tis well I lived
To stop this bloody work !　Deferment played
Into the hands of death.
　　OFFICER.　　　　　Oh, sir, I think
That what begins in honor so should end—

First deeds, not stained, but dusted by the last ;
For, thus the long day of a useful life,
Seems burnished by its close.

HULL. My friend, had all
Been trusty as the men of your command !
But—I am great in silence and shall speak ·
No more of this !   What's done is for the best.

[Retiring.

OFFICER.   A bleached and doting relic of stale time !
His best is bad for us.

*[A squad of Volunteer Militia insultingly surround
the General, hooting and groaning.*

1ST VOLUNTEER. Hull ! hold the fort !
2ND VOLUNTEER. Resist ! We'll back you up !
HULL. Insolent ruffians !
Some men are here in whose sincerity
And courage I have perfect faith—but you !—
Untaught, unmannerly and mutinous—
Your muddy hearts would squirm within your ribs
If I but gave the order to resist!
You would command me ! You who never learned
The simple first note of obedience !
Stand off, nor let me ! I regard you not.
Fine Volunteers are you, who mutinied
O'er such privations as true soldiers laugh at!
Fine Volunteers ! whom we were forced to coax,
And almost drag upon the forest march.
Oh, if I had a thousand more of men,
A thousand less of things—which is your name—
I would defend this Fort, and keep it too.
Stand off and let me pass !

[The GENERAL *walks off.*

1ST VOLUNTEER. The General
Talks well, boys, when he's mad !

Enter an OFFICER.

OFFICER. Fall in ! Fall in !
Here come the British troops—the Fort's surrendered !

Enter GENERAL BROCK *and Forces, with Colors flying and
military music. The American soldiers sullenly ground
arms, and march out of the Fort.*

BROĆK. This is a happy end ! you, Nichol, make—
With Proctor—rough lists of our spoils of war,
Then join with us in grateful prayers to heaven.

[*Exeunt* NICHOL *and* PROCTOR.

Enter TECUMSEH *and* STAYETA *(the latter wearing* BROCK'S
sash) with other Chiefs and Warriors, and LEFROY.

TECUMSEH. My valiant brother is the rising sun—
Our foes the night, which disappears before him !
Our people thank him, and their hearts are his !

BROCK. Why, here is misdirection ! For their thanks—
They fall to you, Tecumseh, more than me !
And, lest what lies in justice should too long
Stand in expectancy—'till thanks seem cold—
Take mine, Tecumseh ! for your services
Have won, with us, the honours of the day,
And you shall share its spoils.

TECUMSEH. Freedom I prize,
And my poor people's welfare more than spoils !
No longer will they wander in the dark ;
The path is open, and the sky is clear.
We thank you for it all !

BROCK. Nay, then, our thanks
We'll interchange—take mine, as I take thine !
But how is this ? Is friendship's gift unused ?
Where is my brother's sash ?—

TECUMSEH. That gift I deemed
Conferred on me as on a warrior,
And, when I saw a worthier than myself,
I could not wear it. 'Tis Stayeta's now—
He keeps it 'till he finds a worthier still.

BROCK. Noble Tecumseh ! thou art still the best !
Men envy their own merit in another—
Grudging e'en what's superfluous to themselves—
But thou—great valour's integer, wouldst share
Its very recompense with all the world !
Here are my pistols— take them from a friend—
Nay—take them !   Would I had a richer gift
To mark my heart's approval of your worth !

Re-enter GENERAL HULL.

HULL. You ask not for my sword—but here it is !
I wielded it in honour in my youth,
And now to yield it, tarnished, in old age,
Vexes me to the soul.
  BROCK.   Then keep it, sir !
  HULL. Trenton and Saratoga speak for me ! (*Aside.*)
I little thought that I should have to knead
In my gray years, this lumpy world again.
But, when my locks were brown, my heart aflame
For liberty, believe me, sir, this sword
Did much to baffle your imperious King !
  BROCK. That stands not in dispute, so keep the sword !
'Tis strange that those who fought for liberty,
Should seek to wrench it from their fellow men.
Impute not guilty war to Kings alone,
Since 'tis the pastime of Republics, too !
Your's has its dreams of glory, conquest, spoil—
Else should we not be here.   But, General,
Wilt dine with us ?   We shall discuss this matter !
  HULL. Nay, let me to my house ; I cannot eat.
  BROCK. Sir, as you will—but prithee, be prepared !
I sail in six days for Niagara,
And you for Montreal.
  HULL.   Till then, adieu !

        [*Exit* GENERAL HULL.

TECUMSEH. Why should my brother leave Detroit so
 soon ?

BROCK. Our foes are massing at Niagara,
And I must meet them; Colonel Proctor stays
In this command.
    TECUMSEH.   I know him very well.
My brother's friend says "go!" but you say "come!"
    BROCK. (*Aside.*) How am I straitened for good officers!
(*To* TECUMSEH.) Friend Proctor's prudence may be use-
    ful here.
    TECUMSEH. I do misgive me o'er my brother's friend.

       Re-enter NICHOL *and* PROCTOR.

    NICHOL. Large stores, munitions, public properties;
A rare account of needed stands of arms;
A brig of war, and military chest—
These are the spoils of bloodless victory.

       [*Handing* GENERAL BROCK *a list.*

    BROCK. Naught is much prized that is not won with
    blood!
    GLEGG. And yet I would old England's victories
Were all as bloodless, ample and complete.
    MACDONELL. O, 'tis a victory fitly gained this day;
Great turning point of our Canadian fortunes!
This day forever should red-lettered stand
In all the calendars of our loved land!

       [*Exeunt.*

GOD SAVE THE QUEEN.

God save our gracious Queen,
Long live our noble Queen,
   God save the Queen ;
Send her victorious,
Happy and glorious,
Long to reign over us ;
   God save the Queen !

O Lord our God, arise,
Scatter her enemies,
   And make them fall !
Confound their politics,
Frustrate their knavish tricks,
On Thee our hopes we fix ;
   God save the Queen !

Thy choicest gifts in store
On her be pleased to pour,
   Long may she reign ;
May she defend our laws,
And ever give us cause
To sing with heart and voice,
   God save the Queen !

HUNTER, ROSE & CO., PRINTERS, TORONTO.